Table of Contents

Our Home 4
Protecting Earth's Water 6
Protecting Earth's Land 10
Protecting Earth's Air 14
How You Can Help 18
Photo Glossary 22
Activity 23
Index 24
After Reading Activity 24
About the Author 24

Our Home

Earth is our home.

People must protect it.

Protecting Earth's Water

Some farms and factories use harmful **chemicals**. They flow into rivers, lakes, and oceans. They make people and animals sick.

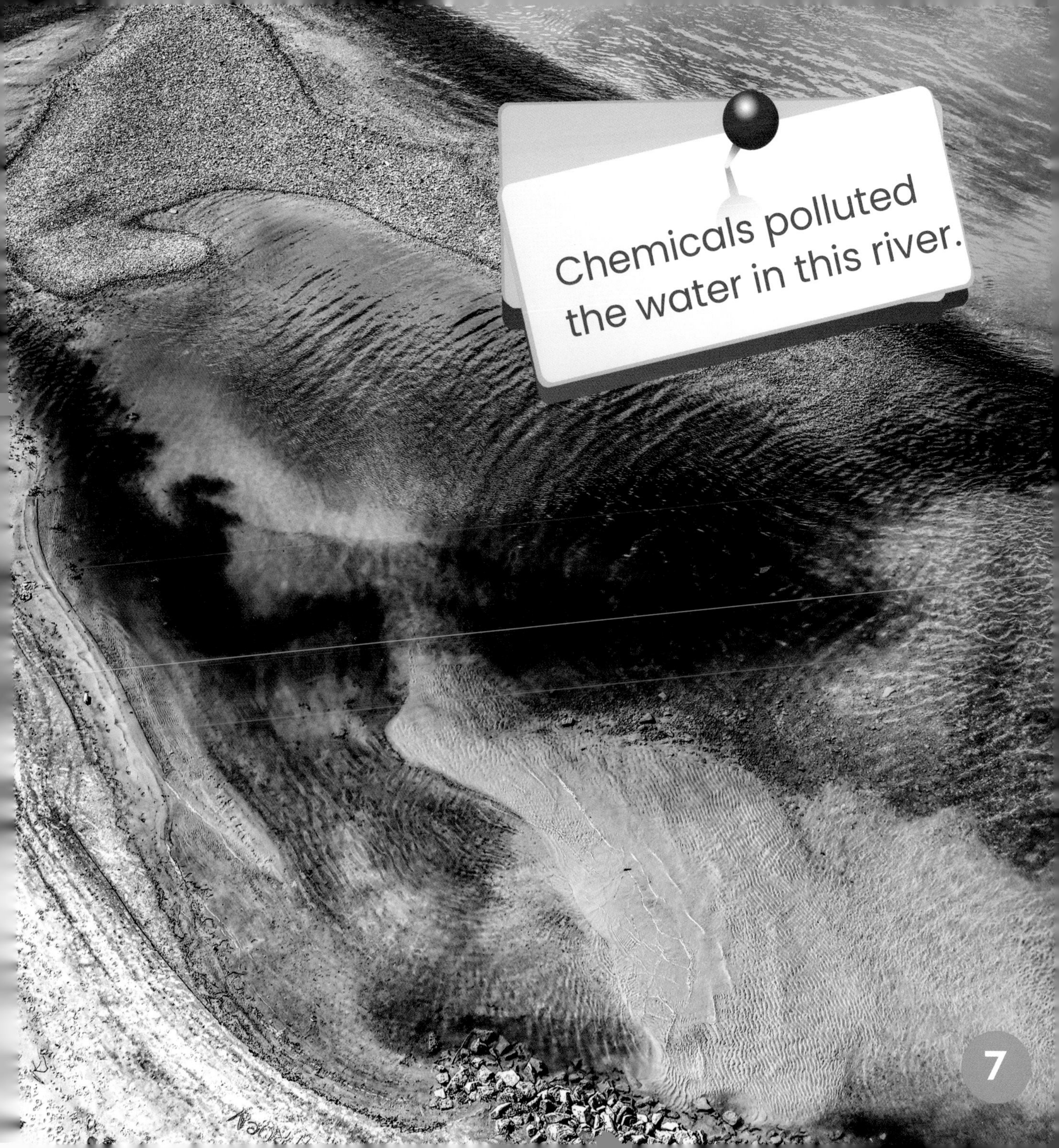

Chemicals polluted the water in this river.

People make rules. The rules say that harmful chemicals are not allowed in the water.

A scientist takes a cup of water to test.

Protecting Earth's Land

Trash **pollutes** Earth's land. It can harm plants and animals.

Some cities have rules about plastic things, such as straws and grocery bags.

People use reusable straws and grocery bags instead. This makes less trash.

Protecting Earth's Air

People burn fuel to make energy. It heats our homes and runs machines. But it also puts harmful **gases** into the air.

There are other ways to make energy. Water, wind, and the sun's rays can make energy.

hydroelectric dam

How You Can Help

You can help protect the Earth!

Recycle and reuse whenever you can. Plant trees to help clean the air. Help keep your community safe and clean.

We can all work together to protect our planet!

HERE IS NO

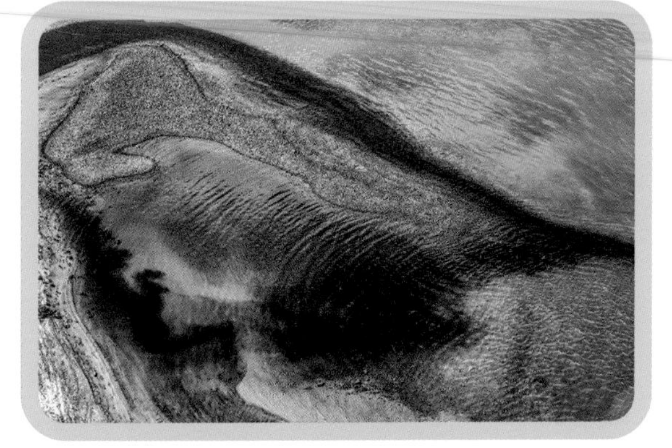

chemicals (KEM-i-kuhlz): Substances made by chemical processes, often in factories.

gases (GAS-ez): Substances that spread to fill any space that contains them.

pollutes (puh-LOOTS): Contaminates with harmful substances such as chemicals, waste, noise, and light.

recycle (ree-SYE-kuhl): To process old items, such as plastic, so that they can be made into new products.

Will It Rot?

Some materials break down in days. Others take thousands of years. Can you guess which of these items will break down first?

Supplies

trowel or small shovel
strips of paper
plastic bottle
food scraps
empty tin can
sticks (4)

Directions

1. With an adult's help, dig four small holes in the ground.
2. Place one item from the list above in each hole. Cover it with soil. Mark it with a stick so you can find it again.
3. Wait two weeks. Then, dig up each item.
4. Observe: Has the item begun to rot? Why or why not?

Index

Earth('s) 4, 6, 10, 14, 18
energy 14, 16
factories 6
plastic 12
trash 10, 13
water 6, 7, 8, 9, 16

About the Author

Lisa J. Amstutz is the author of more than 100 children's books. She loves learning about science and sharing fun facts with kids. Lisa lives on a small farm with her family, two goats, a flock of chickens, and a dog named Daisy.

After Reading Activity

Find out which types of materials can be recycled in your area. Then, look through your pantry. Which food containers can be recycled? Which cannot? How could you cut down on your family's trash?

Library of Congress PCN Data

Protecting Our Planet / Lisa J. Amstutz
(My Earth and Space Science Library)
ISBN (hard cover)(alk. paper) 978-1-73163-844-1
ISBN (soft cover) 978-1-73163-921-9
ISBN (e-Book) 978-1-73163-998-1
ISBN (e-Pub) 978-1-73164-075-8
Library of Congress Control Number: 2020930264

Rourke Educational Media
Printed in the United States of America
01-1942011937

www.rourkeeducationalmedia.com

Edited by: Hailey Scragg
Cover design by: Rhea Magaro-Wallace
Interior design by: Jen Bowers
Photo Credits: Cover logo: frog © Eric Phol, test tube © Sergey Lazarev, p4 © kokouu, p5 © Choreograph, p6 © zhongguo, p7 & p22 © Sorin Opreanu Roberto, p8 © golero, p9 © GregorBister, p10 & p22 © prill, p12, p16 & p22 © narvikk, p13 © Martine Doucet, p14 & p22 © Alexander Gatsenko, p17 © Androsov, p18 © Rawpixel Ltd., p19 © pixelfusion3d, p20 © RapidEye, p21 © Halfpoint , All interior images from istockphoto.com.